# Life and Challenges of IT Professionals

## C. P. Kumar
Reiki Healer & Author
Roorkee - 247667, India

# Disclaimer

While every effort has been made to ensure the accuracy and completeness of the content in this book, the author cannot guarantee that the information contained herein is error-free, up-to-date, or suitable for every individual circumstance.

The author shall not be held liable or responsible for any errors or omissions in the content of the book, nor for any damages, or losses that may arise from any actions taken based upon the suggestions or contents presented in the book.

Readers are advised to use their own judgment and discretion in applying the information provided in this book, and to consult with qualified professionals before taking any action based on the contents of this book. The author disclaims any and all liability or responsibility for any actions taken or not taken based on the information contained in this book.

# DEDICATION

To the indomitable spirit of IT professionals around the world,

This book is dedicated to those who navigate the ever-evolving landscape of technology with resilience, creativity, and a commitment to excellence. It is a tribute to the men and women who have shaped the digital age, facing challenges head-on, and pushing the boundaries of innovation.

In honoring your dedication to mastering the art of technology, this book aspires to illuminate the multifaceted journey of IT professionals. From the roots of the digital era to the complexities of modern cybersecurity, from the delicate balance of work and life to the imperative of diversity and inclusion, each chapter reflects the diverse facets of your professional life.

As we delve into the intricacies of the IT landscape, exploring both triumphs and tribulations, may this book stand as a testament to your unwavering commitment to progress. Your agility, ethical consciousness, and resilience in the face of adversity inspire the narrative within these pages.

To the IT professionals who strive for excellence, embrace change, and contribute not only to the advancement of technology but also to the well-being of society - your dedication is acknowledged and celebrated.

May this book serve as a source of knowledge, inspiration, and reflection for the challenges and victories that define your professional journey. Here's to the IT professionals who shape our digital world and, in doing so, contribute to the collective progress of humanity.

With admiration and gratitude,

C. P. Kumar

# CONTENTS

# PREFACE

In the intricate tapestry of the digital age, this book serves as a guide through the dynamic landscape of the lives and challenges encountered by IT professionals. As we embark on this journey, we unfurl the historical roots of the digital era and its profound influence on our interconnected existence.

The narrative unfolds with the emergence of IT as a profession, tracing its evolution from its nascent stages to its contemporary significance in shaping our world. A panoramic view of the current tech landscape follows, revealing trends, innovations, and disruptive technologies that define the ever-changing digital terrain.

Navigating the complexities of a fast-paced world, we explore the delicate balancing act that IT professionals must perform to maintain equilibrium between their professional responsibilities and personal lives. The exploration of essential skills required in the modern IT landscape reflects the polymathic nature of today's IT professionals.

Adaptability becomes a central theme as we delve into the agile mindset, crucial for success in an environment of rapid technological evolution. The book scrutinizes the evolving challenges of cybersecurity and underscores the pivotal role played by IT professionals in safeguarding the digital realm.

Creativity takes center stage in our discussion of innovation, emphasizing the role of IT professionals in pushing the boundaries of what is possible. Project management methodologies are dissected in the context of IT projects, highlighting the strategic prowess required for successful navigation.

The seismic shift towards remote work prompts an examination of its impact on IT professionals, revealing both challenges and opportunities inherent in this paradigm shift. Ethical considerations are explored, unraveling the complex dilemmas faced by IT professionals in their daily endeavors.

Beyond the technological realm, the book delves into the critical issue of mental health, addressing challenges prevalent in the fast-paced tech industry and proposing strategies for support. The importance of diversity and inclusion in the IT workplace is discussed, shedding light on initiatives aimed at fostering inclusive environments.

Speculating on the future, the book examines emerging roles and potential challenges in the ever-evolving landscape of IT professions. Emphasizing the importance of lifelong learning, we explore strategies for staying abreast of the dynamic industry.

The personal dimension of an IT career is unveiled as we navigate the impact on personal relationships and explore strategies for maintaining a healthy balance. The book concludes by examining the social responsibility of IT professionals, acknowledging their role in addressing societal issues and contributing to positive change.

As readers embark on this odyssey through the multifaceted world of IT professionals, the narrative invites exploration, reflection, and a deeper understanding of the resilience and innovation that define this dynamic field. The book serves as a testament to the unwavering spirit that propels IT professionals forward, shaping the future of our interconnected world.

C. P. Kumar
Reiki Healer & Author
Former Scientist 'G', National Institute of Hydrology
Roorkee - 247667, India
Web: https://www.angelfire.com/nh/cpkumar/virgo.html

In the not-so-distant past, the world operated at a different pace. Analog devices and manual processes defined our daily lives. Then came a transformative era that would reshape the fabric of society - the Digital Age. This chapter serves as a portal into this epoch, laying the foundation for the exploration of the life and challenges faced by IT professionals in an ever-evolving landscape.

**The Evolution of Technology**

The journey into the Digital Age is a tale of remarkable innovation and progress. It begins with the invention of the computer, a colossal leap forward that marked the initiation of a technological revolution. The once-unfathomable capabilities of these machines gradually became woven into the fabric of our existence. From room-sized mainframes to the sleek devices in our pockets, the evolution of technology has been nothing short of extraordinary.

The advent of the internet further accelerated this transformation, connecting people across the globe and ushering in an era of unprecedented communication. The ability to share information instantaneously and on a global scale altered the dynamics of how we work, socialize, and consume information. It laid the groundwork for the interconnected world we navigate today.

**Impact on Daily Lives**

As technology became an integral part of our daily lives, it brought about profound changes. The way we communicate, work, and entertain ourselves underwent a seismic shift. Smartphones became extensions of ourselves, providing access to a universe of information at our fingertips. Social media platforms emerged, shaping the way we build and maintain relationships.

In the realm of work, the Digital Age birthed a new paradigm. Traditional office spaces transformed into digital landscapes, enabling remote collaboration and flexible work arrangements. The concept of a 9-to-5 workday gave way to a more fluid, always-connected work environment.

## Challenges in the Digital Era

With these advancements came a set of challenges that were previously unimaginable. The rapid pace of technological change left many struggling to adapt. As our lives became increasingly intertwined with digital platforms, concerns about privacy, security, and the ethical implications of technology emerged.

The Digital Age also brought about a paradoxical relationship with time. While technology promised to make tasks more efficient, it also created an environment where the line between work and personal life blurred. The constant connectivity fostered a culture of always being "on", raising questions about the sustainability of this lifestyle.

## The Unfolding Tapestry of IT Professionals' Lives

As we delve into the lives of IT professionals, it becomes evident that they are the architects of this digital realm. They are the ones tasked with navigating the complexities of an ever-evolving tech landscape. From programming and network management to cybersecurity and innovation, IT professionals play a pivotal role in shaping the contours of the Digital Age.

The challenges they face extend beyond technical expertise. IT professionals find themselves at the intersection of innovation and responsibility. As the gatekeepers of digital systems, they grapple with the weighty responsibility of safeguarding data and ensuring the ethical use of technology.

**Looking Ahead: Navigating the Unknown**

As we stand on the threshold of the Digital Age, the journey ahead is both thrilling and uncertain. The rapid evolution of technology promises exciting possibilities, yet it demands constant adaptation. In the chapters that follow, we will unravel the intricacies of the life of an IT professional - their rise in prominence, the skills required to thrive, the challenges they confront, and the ethical dilemmas they navigate.

This book is a testament to the resilience and creativity of those who inhabit the world of information technology. It is a guide for both seasoned professionals and those embarking on a career in the ever-expanding realm of IT. Join us as we embark on a journey through the digital corridors that shape our present and define our future.

## Introduction

The rapid advancement of technology in the 21$^{st}$ century has brought about a monumental shift in the professional landscape, with Information Technology (IT) emerging as a cornerstone of modern business and society. The rise of the IT professional is a captivating tale that unfolds through the annals of history, reflecting the dynamic interplay between human ingenuity and technological innovation. In this article, we will traverse the evolution of IT as a profession, exploring its roots, milestones, and the challenges faced by those who navigate the ever-evolving landscape of digital transformation.

## Genesis of IT as a Profession

The seeds of the IT profession were sown in the mid-20$^{th}$ century, a time when computers were colossal machines housed in air-conditioned rooms and operated by a select cadre of experts. During this era, the role of the computer scientist or systems analyst emerged, laying the groundwork for the IT professional. Their primary responsibilities included designing algorithms, programming languages, and developing the first rudimentary software systems.

## The Advent of Personal Computing

The 1970s witnessed a seismic shift with the introduction of personal computers, bringing computing power to the masses. This democratization of technology marked a pivotal moment in the evolution of IT, as individuals began to explore the vast potential of computing in their homes and workplaces. The role of the IT professional expanded to encompass network administration, software development, and user support.

## The Internet Revolution

As the world entered the 1990s, the Internet revolutionized the IT landscape. The advent of the World Wide Web transformed the way information was accessed and shared, giving rise to a new breed of IT professionals – web developers, system administrators, and cybersecurity experts. The demand for skilled IT professionals surged, with organizations recognizing the strategic importance of a robust online presence.

## The Dot-Com Boom and Bust

The late 1990s saw the dot-com boom, characterized by a frenzy of internet-based startups. IT professionals became the driving force behind these enterprises, leading to unprecedented demand for their skills. However, the euphoria was short-lived as the dot-com bubble burst in the early 2000s, leading to a temporary downturn in the IT job market. This period served as a crucible, testing the resilience of IT professionals and paving the way for a more mature and sustainable industry.

## Globalization and Outsourcing

The 21$^{st}$ century brought with it the era of globalization, transforming the IT profession into a global phenomenon. Companies sought to harness the advantages of cost-effective labor, leading to the outsourcing of IT services to countries with a burgeoning pool of skilled professionals. This shift posed challenges for IT professionals in traditional hubs, necessitating adaptability and a broader skill set to remain competitive in an increasingly interconnected world.

## Mobile Technology and the App Economy

The proliferation of smartphones and mobile applications in the late 2000s sparked a new wave of innovation. IT professionals found themselves at the forefront of this mobile revolution, developing apps that became integral to daily life. The app economy not only created new career opportunities but also redefined the skill set required for success in the IT industry.

## Cloud Computing and Virtualization

Cloud Computing is a technology that provides on-demand access to a shared pool of computing resources (such as servers, storage, and applications) over the internet, enabling scalable and flexible services. Virtualization is a technology that creates virtual instances of computing resources (such as servers, storage, or networks) to maximize efficiency, resource utilization, and flexibility in IT infrastructure.

In recent years, cloud computing and virtualization have emerged as transformative forces in the IT landscape. IT professionals now grapple with the challenges and opportunities presented by the shift towards cloud-based infrastructure and services. The ability to navigate and optimize cloud environments has become a coveted skill, underlining the dynamic nature of the IT profession.

## Big Data and Analytics

Big Data refers to large volumes of structured and unstructured data that cannot be easily processed by traditional database systems, while Analytics involves the use of mathematical and statistical techniques to analyze and interpret data, uncovering meaningful insights and supporting decision-making.

The exponential growth of data has given rise to the field of big data and analytics. IT professionals are at the forefront of harnessing the power of data to derive insights, drive decision-making, and fuel innovation. This evolution underscores the adaptability of IT professionals, who continually embrace new technologies to stay relevant in an ever-changing landscape.

**Cybersecurity Challenges**

As technology advances, so do the threats associated with it. Cybersecurity has become a paramount concern, and IT professionals play a crucial role in safeguarding digital assets against malicious actors. The constant cat-and-mouse game between security experts and cybercriminals highlights the need for IT professionals to stay abreast of evolving security threats and countermeasures.

**The Future of IT Professionals**

Looking ahead, the future promises continued evolution and challenges for IT professionals. Emerging technologies such as artificial intelligence, quantum computing, and the Internet of Things will reshape the IT landscape, presenting both opportunities and complexities. IT professionals will need to embrace lifelong learning, adaptability, and a proactive approach to stay at the forefront of innovation.

**Conclusion**

The rise of the IT professional is an extraordinary journey marked by innovation, resilience, and adaptability. From the early days of room-sized computers to the current era of cloud computing and big data, IT professionals have been at the vanguard of technological progress. As we navigate the future, the challenges faced by IT professionals will undoubtedly evolve, but their role as architects of the digital age remains paramount. The story of the IT professional is a testament to the indomitable spirit of human curiosity and the relentless pursuit of knowledge, underscoring their indispensable role in shaping the world we live in today.

## Introduction

In the rapidly evolving realm of technology, the life of IT professionals is a perpetual journey marked by challenges and opportunities. The tech landscape is a dynamic terrain, shaped by trends, innovations, and disruptive technologies that demand constant adaptation. This article delves into the current state of technology, offering insights into the multifaceted world IT professionals inhabit.

## Rapid Technological Advancements

The tech landscape is characterized by relentless progress, with advancements unfolding at an unprecedented pace. From artificial intelligence (AI) and machine learning to quantum computing, IT professionals find themselves at the forefront of groundbreaking developments. The sheer speed of innovation presents both exhilarating possibilities and daunting challenges.

## AI and Machine Learning

Artificial Intelligence (AI) refers to the development of computer systems that can perform tasks that typically require human intelligence, while Machine Learning (ML) is a subset of AI that focuses on enabling systems to learn and improve from experience without explicit programming, using algorithms and statistical models.

Artificial Intelligence and Machine Learning have emerged as pivotal forces, transforming industries and redefining the IT landscape. As algorithms become more sophisticated, IT professionals are tasked with harnessing the power of AI to enhance efficiency, automate processes, and unlock new realms of creativity. However, ethical considerations and the fear of job displacement underscore the challenges associated with these technologies.

**Data Privacy and Cybersecurity**

The proliferation of digital data has given rise to heightened concerns regarding data privacy and cybersecurity. IT professionals are entrusted with safeguarding sensitive information in an era of increasing cyber threats. The battle against cybercriminals is a perpetual challenge, requiring IT experts to stay one step ahead through innovative security measures and a comprehensive understanding of evolving threat landscapes.

**Cloud Computing**

Cloud computing has revolutionized the way organizations manage and store data. IT professionals are integral to the adoption and optimization of cloud solutions, ensuring scalability, accessibility, and security. The shift to cloud-based infrastructures necessitates a skill set that blends traditional IT expertise with an understanding of cloud architecture.

**Internet of Things (IoT)**

The interconnected web of devices known as the Internet of Things has permeated our daily lives and business operations. IT professionals play a pivotal role in navigating the complexities of IoT, addressing challenges related to data integration, interoperability, and security. As IoT continues to expand, IT experts must possess a holistic understanding of hardware, software, and connectivity.

**Blockchain Technology**

Blockchain technology is a decentralized and distributed ledger system that securely records and verifies transactions across a network of computers, providing transparency, immutability, and cryptographic security.

Blockchain, initially synonymous with cryptocurrencies, has evolved into a transformative technology with applications across various industries. IT professionals are tasked with harnessing the potential of decentralized and secure ledgers, revolutionizing processes such as supply chain management, finance, and healthcare. However, the integration of blockchain comes with its own set of challenges, including regulatory hurdles and interoperability concerns.

**Remote Work and Collaboration Tools**

Remote work, also known as telecommuting or telework, refers to the practice of working outside a traditional office environment, often enabled by technology such as internet connectivity and collaborative tools, allowing employees to perform their job tasks from various locations, such as home or co-working spaces.

The paradigm shift towards remote work has become a defining feature of the tech landscape, accelerated by global events. IT professionals are instrumental in facilitating seamless collaboration through the deployment and optimization of communication tools, project management platforms, and virtual workspaces. Balancing the benefits of remote work with the challenges of maintaining security and connectivity is an ongoing task.

## Disruptive Technologies

Disruptive technologies are innovations that significantly alter or revolutionize industries by introducing new approaches, products, or services, often rendering existing technologies or business models obsolete and reshaping the competitive landscape.

Innovation often comes in the form of disruptive technologies that challenge existing paradigms. From 5G connectivity to *edge computing*, IT professionals find themselves navigating uncharted territory. The integration of these technologies requires a proactive approach, as well as the ability to anticipate and mitigate potential disruptions.

Edge computing is a distributed computing paradigm where data processing is performed closer to the source of data generation or the "edge" of the network, rather than relying solely on centralized cloud servers. This approach reduces latency, enhances real-time processing capabilities, and can be particularly useful for applications that require quick response times, such as IoT devices and certain industrial processes.

## Skill Diversification and Continuous Learning

The dynamic nature of the tech landscape demands a commitment to continuous learning and skill diversification. IT professionals must embrace a mindset of perpetual education, staying abreast of emerging technologies and adapting their skill sets accordingly. The ability to pivot and acquire new skills swiftly is essential in a field where obsolescence is a constant threat.

**Ethical Considerations in Technology**

As technology permeates every facet of our lives, ethical considerations loom large. IT professionals are confronted with decisions that transcend technical proficiency, requiring a nuanced understanding of the societal impact of their work. Issues such as bias in algorithms, privacy concerns, and the responsible use of emerging technologies necessitate a robust ethical framework within the IT profession.

**Conclusion**

The tech landscape is a vast and ever-changing terrain that demands resilience, adaptability, and a relentless pursuit of knowledge from IT professionals. Navigating the challenges and embracing the opportunities embedded in this dynamic environment is not merely a professional obligation but a journey that defines the very essence of the IT profession. As technology continues to evolve, so too will the role of IT professionals, shaping the future of the digital age.

## Introduction

In the fast-paced world of technology, where the rhythm of innovation beats incessantly, IT professionals find themselves caught in a perpetual balancing act. The demands of the digital age, coupled with the ever-evolving landscape of their profession, make striking a harmonious chord between work and life a formidable challenge. This article explores the multifaceted challenges that IT professionals encounter in maintaining a work-life balance, shedding light on the impact of the always-connected digital world on their personal and professional lives.

## The Pervasive Nature of Connectivity

One of the primary challenges faced by IT professionals is the pervasive nature of connectivity. In an era where smartphones and laptops serve as extensions of the self, boundaries between work and personal life blur. The ability to respond to emails, attend virtual meetings, and troubleshoot issues remotely means that the traditional 9-to-5 work structure has become a relic of the past. As IT professionals find themselves tethered to their devices, the distinction between professional obligations and personal time dissolves.

## The 24/7 Work Culture

The advent of globalization has ushered in a 24/7 work culture, wherein IT professionals are expected to be available around the clock. The global nature of many IT projects means that teams are dispersed across different time zones, necessitating constant communication and collaboration. While this interconnectedness enhances productivity and facilitates timely decision-making, it also encroaches on the personal time of IT professionals. Juggling work commitments with family responsibilities becomes a delicate act as the demands of the digital world transcend temporal boundaries.

## Impact on Mental Well-being

The incessant connectivity and the pressure to meet tight deadlines take a toll on the mental well-being of IT professionals. The constant stream of information, coupled with the expectation of immediate responses, contributes to high levels of stress and burnout. The boundaryless work environment leaves little room for relaxation and rejuvenation, leading to fatigue and diminished job satisfaction. In the quest to stay ahead in the competitive IT landscape, professionals often sacrifice their mental well-being, inadvertently compromising the quality of both their personal and professional lives.

## Striking a Balance: Strategies and Techniques

While the challenges are undeniable, IT professionals are not powerless in the face of an always-connected digital world. Adopting effective strategies and techniques can help strike a balance between work and life.

### 1. Establishing Boundaries

Setting clear boundaries between work and personal life is essential. IT professionals should define specific times for work-related activities and commit to respecting their personal time. This might involve creating designated workspaces at home or turning off email notifications during non-working hours.

## 2. Prioritizing Self-Care

Prioritizing self-care is crucial for maintaining resilience in the face of constant demands. Regular exercise, sufficient sleep, and mindfulness practices can help mitigate stress and improve overall well-being. IT professionals must recognize that taking care of themselves is not a luxury but a necessity for sustained success in their careers.

## 3. Effective Time Management

Effective time management is a skill that becomes even more critical in the IT field. Prioritizing tasks, setting realistic deadlines, and delegating responsibilities can help IT professionals optimize their work hours. By being intentional about how time is allocated, professionals can achieve greater productivity without sacrificing personal time.

## 4. Communication and Negotiation

Open communication with employers and colleagues is key to finding a workable balance. IT professionals should feel empowered to negotiate realistic workloads, deadlines, and expectations. Creating a culture of understanding and flexibility within the workplace can contribute to a healthier work-life equilibrium.

**The Role of Organizations**

While individual efforts are indispensable, organizations also play a pivotal role in fostering a work environment that supports a healthy work-life balance for IT professionals.

# 1. Flexible Work Arrangements

Organizations can embrace flexible work arrangements, such as remote work options or flexible hours. This flexibility empowers IT professionals to structure their work in a way that accommodates personal commitments and promotes a better work-life balance.

# 2. Employee Support Programs

Implementing employee support programs, including mental health resources and counseling services, demonstrates a commitment to the well-being of IT professionals. Providing access to resources that address stress and burnout can contribute to a more resilient and satisfied workforce.

# 3. Redefining Success Metrics

Shifting the focus from sheer hours worked to outcomes achieved can redefine success metrics in the IT industry. Recognizing and rewarding efficiency and innovation rather than sheer time commitment can contribute to a healthier work culture.

# 4. Encouraging a Healthy Work Culture

Organizations can foster a healthy work culture by discouraging excessive overtime, promoting regular breaks, and encouraging employees to take their allotted vacation time. A workplace that values work-life balance is more likely to attract and retain top IT talent.

**Conclusion**

In the dynamic and fast-paced world of IT, the challenge of balancing work and life is an ongoing journey. IT professionals must navigate the digital landscape with resilience, adopting strategies that preserve their mental well-being and foster a harmonious integration of personal and professional spheres. Organizations, in turn, have a responsibility to create environments that prioritize the holistic well-being of their workforce. As the digital age continues to evolve, the pursuit of a balanced life remains an imperative for IT professionals seeking sustained success and fulfillment in their careers.

## Introduction

In the ever-evolving landscape of Information Technology (IT), professionals are faced with unprecedented challenges and opportunities. The rapid pace of technological advancements demands a versatile skill set from IT professionals to stay relevant and thrive in their careers. This article delves into the essential skills and competencies required in today's dynamic IT environment, exploring the multifaceted aspects that make a modern IT professional successful.

## Technical Proficiency

At the core of an IT professional's skill set lies technical proficiency. The ability to understand and leverage cutting-edge technologies is non-negotiable. In today's IT landscape, where cloud computing, artificial intelligence, and cybersecurity are paramount, professionals must continually update their technical knowledge. This includes staying abreast of the latest programming languages, frameworks, and tools relevant to their field.

The modern IT professional should be adept at working with cloud platforms such as AWS, Azure, or Google Cloud. Moreover, a comprehensive understanding of machine learning, data analytics, and cybersecurity is crucial to navigate the complexities of contemporary IT projects.

## Adaptability and Continuous Learning

The IT industry is synonymous with change. Technologies that were considered groundbreaking yesterday may become obsolete tomorrow. In this environment, adaptability and a commitment to continuous learning are indispensable skills. IT professionals need to embrace change, proactively seek new knowledge, and be willing to unlearn and relearn as technology evolves.

Keeping up with industry trends, attending workshops, earning certifications, and participating in online courses are essential for staying ahead. The ability to quickly adapt to new methodologies and paradigms ensures that IT professionals remain valuable assets to their organizations.

## Problem-Solving and Critical Thinking

Beyond technical prowess, the modern IT professional must excel in problem-solving and critical thinking. As technology becomes more integrated into business processes, IT professionals are often tasked with solving complex problems that require a combination of technical expertise and analytical thinking. Whether troubleshooting system issues, optimizing processes, or designing innovative solutions, the ability to think critically is key.

Problem-solving also involves effective communication and collaboration. IT professionals must be able to translate technical jargon into layman's terms, enabling effective communication with non-technical stakeholders. Additionally, collaboration with cross-functional teams is crucial to develop holistic solutions that align with broader organizational goals.

## Communication and Interpersonal Skills

Contrary to the stereotype of the solitary coder hidden in a dark room, the modern IT professional needs strong communication and interpersonal skills. The ability to convey complex technical concepts to non-technical stakeholders is paramount. Whether presenting ideas to management, collaborating with colleagues, or providing support to end-users, effective communication ensures that IT initiatives are well-understood and aligned with organizational objectives.

Interpersonal skills are equally crucial, especially as IT professionals often work in multidisciplinary teams. Building strong relationships with team members, stakeholders, and clients fosters collaboration and ensures the success of IT projects. Moreover, interpersonal skills contribute to a positive work environment, enhancing job satisfaction and productivity.

## Project Management and Time Management

In the fast-paced world of IT, project management skills are invaluable. IT professionals are frequently engaged in projects that have tight deadlines and complex requirements. The ability to plan, execute, and monitor projects efficiently is crucial for success.

Time management is a subset of project management but deserves special attention. Juggling multiple tasks and priorities is common in IT roles. Professionals must prioritize effectively, allocate resources wisely, and meet deadlines without compromising on quality. Effective time management ensures that IT projects are delivered on time and within budget.

## Cybersecurity Awareness

As technology advances, so do the threats associated with it. Cybersecurity is a top priority for organizations across industries. Modern IT professionals must be well-versed in cybersecurity best practices, understanding the potential risks and implementing measures to safeguard sensitive information.

This involves knowledge of encryption protocols, network security, and awareness of social engineering tactics. Moreover, staying informed about the latest cybersecurity threats and trends is essential to proactively protect systems and data from evolving risks.

## Emotional Intelligence

In a profession that often involves problem-solving and collaboration, emotional intelligence is a valuable asset. The ability to understand and manage one's emotions, as well as navigate the emotions of others, contributes to effective teamwork and leadership. IT professionals with high emotional intelligence can handle stressful situations, build positive relationships, and foster a supportive work culture.

## Conclusion

The life and challenges of IT professionals are intricately linked to their skill set. In today's dynamic landscape, a successful IT professional is more than just a technical expert. The blend of technical proficiency, adaptability, critical thinking, communication skills, project management acumen, cybersecurity awareness, and emotional intelligence defines the modern IT professional.

As the IT industry continues to evolve, professionals must prioritize continuous learning and development to stay relevant. Embracing a holistic approach to skills development ensures that IT professionals not only meet the demands of their current roles but also position themselves for success in the challenges of tomorrow. The journey of an IT professional is a continuous learning experience, and those who navigate it with agility and a comprehensive skill set are well-equipped to thrive in the ever-changing world of technology.

## Introduction

In the ever-evolving landscape of Information Technology (IT), professionals find themselves navigating a dynamic and challenging terrain. The pace of change, technological advancements, and the demand for innovation require IT experts to cultivate a mindset that goes beyond technical proficiency. This article explores the significance of the Agile Mindset in the lives of IT professionals, emphasizing its role in fostering adaptability, resilience, and continuous improvement.

## Understanding the Agile Mindset

The Agile Mindset refers to a set of values, principles, and practices emphasizing flexibility, collaboration, and continuous improvement in the development and delivery of projects or products. It emphasizes adaptability, customer satisfaction, and iterative development processes, commonly associated with Agile methodologies such as Scrum and Kanban in the software development industry.

Scrum is an Agile framework with fixed-length iterations and defined roles, ceremonies, and artifacts for software development and project management. Kanban is a flow-based Agile methodology without fixed iterations, emphasizing continuous delivery and visualizing work on a board.

The Agile Mindset is a set of principles and values derived from the Agile Manifesto, originally formulated for software development. However, its applicability extends far beyond coding and project management; it permeates the essence of how IT professionals approach challenges, collaborate with teams, and respond to the ever-changing demands of the industry.

## 1. Agility in the Face of Change

Change is the only constant in the IT industry. Technologies evolve, frameworks shift, and methodologies transform. The Agile Mindset equips IT professionals with the ability to embrace change rather than resist it. Instead of viewing change as a disruption, an agile mindset sees it as an opportunity for growth and improvement.

By understanding that change is inevitable, IT professionals can adopt a proactive approach, staying ahead of industry trends and acquiring new skills. This mindset encourages a culture of continuous learning, enabling professionals to adapt swiftly to emerging technologies and methodologies.

## 2. Collaboration and Cross-Functional Teams

The collaborative nature of the Agile Mindset is a key element in the success of IT professionals. In an industry where teamwork is paramount, an agile mindset fosters effective communication, trust, and collaboration. Cross-functional teams, consisting of individuals with diverse skills and expertise, work together seamlessly to achieve common goals.

Breaking down silos and promoting open communication not only enhances the quality of deliverables but also creates an environment where ideas flow freely. IT professionals operating with an agile mindset understand that the collective intelligence of a team surpasses individual brilliance. This collaborative spirit is vital in addressing complex challenges and delivering innovative solutions.


## 3. Iterative Development and Continuous Improvement

Central to the Agile Mindset is the concept of iterative development. Instead of adhering to rigid, long-term plans, IT professionals embrace an iterative approach that allows for flexibility and adaptability. This methodology, often associated with Agile frameworks like Scrum, emphasizes the delivery of small, incremental improvements.

By focusing on delivering functional increments regularly, IT professionals can obtain feedback early and often, ensuring that the final product meets the evolving needs of stakeholders. This iterative cycle not only enhances the quality of the deliverable but also facilitates continuous improvement. IT professionals with an agile mindset are constantly seeking ways to refine processes, optimize workflows, and enhance overall efficiency.

**Adopting the Agile Mindset in IT**

## 1. Cultivating a Learning Culture

One of the cornerstones of the Agile Mindset is a commitment to lifelong learning. IT professionals must actively seek opportunities to acquire new skills, stay informed about industry trends, and expand their knowledge base. This commitment to learning not only enhances individual capabilities but also contributes to the collective growth of teams and organizations.

Encouraging a learning culture involves providing resources for training and development, fostering mentorship programs, and creating an environment where mistakes are viewed as opportunities for learning and improvement. The agile mindset recognizes that knowledge is a dynamic asset, and the ability to learn and adapt is a key factor in long-term success.

## 2. Embracing Failure as a Stepping Stone

In the pursuit of innovation, failures are inevitable. The agile mindset encourages IT professionals to view failure not as a setback but as a valuable learning experience. By embracing failure and treating it as a stepping stone to success, individuals and teams can foster resilience and develop the ability to bounce back from challenges.

Organizations that promote a culture of psychological safety, where individuals feel comfortable taking risks and sharing their failures, create an environment conducive to innovation. The agile mindset recognizes that innovation often emerges from the lessons learned through failure, leading to more robust solutions and breakthroughs.

## 3. Prioritizing Customer Value and Feedback

At the heart of the Agile Mindset is a commitment to delivering value to the customer. IT professionals must prioritize understanding the needs and expectations of their customers and stakeholders. By maintaining a customer-centric focus, professionals can align their efforts with business objectives and ensure that the delivered solutions meet real-world requirements.

Continuous feedback loops are integral to the agile mindset. Soliciting feedback early and regularly from customers and end-users allows IT professionals to make informed adjustments, ensuring that the final product aligns with expectations. This customer-driven approach not only enhances the quality of deliverables but also fosters a sense of partnership between IT teams and their clients.

## Conclusion

In the dynamic realm of IT, the Agile Mindset serves as a compass, guiding professionals through the challenges of an ever-changing landscape. Its principles of adaptability, collaboration, and continuous improvement empower IT professionals to thrive in an industry where agility is not just an advantage but a necessity.

By embracing the Agile Mindset, IT professionals can navigate the complexities of their profession with resilience and innovation. Cultivating a learning culture, embracing failure as a stepping stone, and prioritizing customer value are essential components of adopting this mindset. As the IT industry continues to evolve, those with an agile mindset will not only endure but also lead the way in shaping the future of technology and its impact on our lives.

## Introduction

In the fast-paced and ever-evolving realm of information technology, IT professionals find themselves at the forefront of a digital battleground. As the world becomes increasingly interconnected, the challenges associated with cybersecurity have grown exponentially. This article delves into the intricate landscape of cybersecurity threats, exploring the dynamic nature of the field and the pivotal role IT professionals play in safeguarding digital assets.

## The Evolving Cybersecurity Landscape

The digital era has ushered in unprecedented opportunities and conveniences, but it has also given rise to a myriad of cybersecurity threats. From traditional malware to sophisticated phishing schemes and ransomware attacks, the threat landscape is constantly evolving. As technology advances, so do the tactics employed by cybercriminals. IT professionals are tasked with staying one step ahead, anticipating and mitigating potential threats to protect the integrity of digital infrastructures.

### 1. Advanced Persistent Threats (APTs)

One of the prominent challenges faced by IT professionals is the rise of Advanced Persistent Threats (APTs). These are stealthy and continuous cyberattacks orchestrated by highly organized groups or nation-states with the intent of gaining unauthorized access to sensitive information. APTs often employ sophisticated techniques, such as *zero-day exploits* (cyber attacks that target software vulnerabilities on the same day they are discovered, exploiting security flaws before developers or vendors can release patches or countermeasures) and social engineering, making them difficult to detect and mitigate.

## 2. Ransomware Attacks

Ransomware is a type of malicious software that encrypts a victim's files or systems, rendering them inaccessible, and demands payment in exchange for the decryption key or to prevent the release of sensitive information.

Ransomware has become a pervasive and financially lucrative form of cybercrime. IT professionals grapple with the constant evolution of ransomware tactics, from encrypting files to exploiting vulnerabilities in critical infrastructure. The implications of a successful ransomware attack can be severe, ranging from financial loss to reputational damage. The cat-and-mouse game between cybercriminals and IT professionals requires a proactive and adaptive approach to cybersecurity.

## 3. Internet of Things (IoT) Vulnerabilities

The Internet of Things (IoT) refers to the network of interconnected physical devices, vehicles, appliances, and other objects embedded with sensors, software, and connectivity, enabling them to collect and exchange data over the internet.

The proliferation of IoT devices adds another layer of complexity to the cybersecurity landscape. With the interconnectivity of devices ranging from smart home appliances to industrial control systems, the attack surface for cybercriminals widens. IT professionals must grapple with securing diverse and often resource-constrained IoT devices, ensuring they are not exploited to gain unauthorized access to networks.

## The Role of IT Professionals in Cybersecurity

As the digital landscape continues to evolve, the role of IT professionals in ensuring robust cybersecurity has become more critical than ever. These professionals serve as the first line of defense against cyber threats, employing a combination of technical expertise, strategic thinking, and continuous learning.

### 1. Threat Detection and Prevention

One of the primary responsibilities of IT professionals is the timely detection and prevention of cybersecurity threats. This involves implementing robust security measures, deploying intrusion detection systems, and leveraging artificial intelligence and machine learning for anomaly detection. By staying vigilant and proactive, IT professionals can thwart potential attacks before they cause significant damage.

### 2. Incident Response and Mitigation

Despite the best preventive measures, cybersecurity incidents are inevitable. IT professionals must be adept at developing and implementing incident response plans. This involves swift identification of the nature and scope of the breach, containment of the incident, and the restoration of affected systems. A well-defined incident response strategy is crucial for minimizing the impact of cyberattacks and facilitating a swift recovery.

## 3. Continuous Monitoring and Adaptation

Cybersecurity is a dynamic field, requiring IT professionals to engage in continuous monitoring and adaptation. This involves staying abreast of emerging threats, regularly updating security protocols, and conducting penetration testing to identify vulnerabilities. The ability to adapt to the evolving nature of cybersecurity threats is a hallmark of effective IT professionals.

## 4. User Education and Awareness

Human error remains a significant factor in cybersecurity incidents. IT professionals play a pivotal role in educating users about cybersecurity best practices and raising awareness about potential threats. This includes training employees to recognize phishing attempts, promoting the use of strong passwords, and fostering a culture of cybersecurity consciousness within organizations.

## 5. Regulatory Compliance and Data Privacy

The regulatory landscape surrounding cybersecurity is constantly evolving, with laws and compliance standards becoming increasingly stringent. IT professionals must navigate this complex terrain, ensuring that organizations adhere to relevant regulations and standards. This includes safeguarding sensitive data, implementing encryption measures, and being prepared for audits to demonstrate compliance.

**Challenges Faced by IT Professionals**

While IT professionals are at the forefront of cybersecurity defense, they face numerous challenges in their mission to protect digital assets and information. These challenges range from resource constraints to the evolving sophistication of cyber threats.

## 1. Resource Constraints

Many organizations, particularly smaller ones, may face resource constraints that limit their ability to invest in robust cybersecurity measures. IT professionals often find themselves working within tight budgets, necessitating creative solutions to maximize the impact of available resources. Balancing the need for security with budgetary constraints is a constant challenge in the life of IT professionals.

## 2. Skills Gap

The field of cybersecurity is dynamic, and the demand for skilled professionals far exceeds the supply. IT professionals must continually update their skills to keep pace with emerging threats and technologies. The skills gap poses a significant challenge, as organizations struggle to find and retain qualified cybersecurity experts. This underscores the importance of investing in training and professional development within the IT sector.

## 3. Insider Threats

While external threats often take the spotlight, insider threats pose a significant risk to cybersecurity. IT professionals must navigate the delicate balance between enabling employees to perform their duties and safeguarding against malicious or unintentional insider actions. This challenge involves implementing robust access controls, monitoring user activities, and fostering a culture of trust and accountability within organizations.

4. Complexity of IT Infrastructures

The increasing complexity of IT infrastructures, including *hybrid cloud environments* (combination of private and public cloud infrastructures, allowing data and applications to be shared between them) and interconnected networks, adds a layer of difficulty for IT professionals. Managing and securing diverse systems and technologies require a comprehensive understanding of the entire ecosystem. The challenge lies in implementing cohesive security measures that address the intricacies of modern IT architectures.

**Conclusion**

In the dynamic and interconnected world of information technology, cybersecurity challenges are omnipresent. IT professionals find themselves at the forefront, navigating a complex landscape of evolving threats and rapidly advancing technologies. The role of these professionals in safeguarding digital assets is pivotal, encompassing threat detection, incident response, continuous adaptation, user education, and regulatory compliance.

Despite the challenges they face, IT professionals remain resilient and adaptive, employing a combination of technical expertise and strategic thinking to stay ahead of cyber threats. As the digital landscape continues to evolve, the life of IT professionals will be marked by an ongoing commitment to securing the digital realm and mitigating the risks posed by an ever-expanding array of cyber threats.

**Introduction**

In the fast-paced realm of Information Technology (IT), professionals find themselves at the forefront of innovation and creativity. In a world that constantly demands advancements, IT professionals play a pivotal role in shaping the future. This article delves into the dynamic relationship between innovation, creativity, and IT professionals, exploring how their contributions drive progress and overcome the challenges in this ever-evolving industry.

**The Nexus of Innovation and IT**

1. Innovation as a Catalyst for Change

At the heart of the IT industry lies the spirit of innovation. IT professionals are tasked with harnessing the power of emerging technologies to solve complex problems and streamline processes. From artificial intelligence to blockchain and cloud computing, the IT landscape is marked by a continuous influx of novel ideas that propel the industry forward.

Innovation in IT is not merely about adopting the latest technology but about envisioning new possibilities and pushing boundaries. IT professionals serve as the architects of this change, driving the adoption of cutting-edge solutions that redefine how businesses operate and how individuals interact with technology.

## 2. Creativity: The Fuel for Progress

While innovation is often associated with technological breakthroughs, creativity is the catalyst that fuels the process. IT professionals need to think beyond conventional solutions and imagine new ways to address challenges. Creativity enables them to design intuitive user interfaces, develop novel algorithms, and devise innovative strategies to tackle cybersecurity threats.

The IT industry is not immune to routine challenges, and creativity becomes the differentiating factor when it comes to problem-solving. Creative thinking allows IT professionals to approach issues from unconventional angles, leading to breakthroughs that might have eluded a more rigid mindset.

## The Role of IT Professionals in Fostering Innovation

### 1. Adopting a Mindset of Continuous Learning

Innovation thrives in an environment where learning is a constant. IT professionals need to embrace a mindset of continuous learning to stay abreast of the latest developments in technology. The ever-expanding landscape of IT demands professionals who are not only proficient in existing technologies but are also eager to explore and adapt to new ones.

Continuous learning opens avenues for IT professionals to experiment with emerging tools and methodologies, fostering a culture where innovation is not only welcomed but actively pursued. As they delve into the depths of new technologies, IT professionals become the driving force behind the industry's transformative journey.

## 2. Nurturing a Collaborative Culture

Innovation seldom occurs in isolation. IT professionals thrive in environments that encourage collaboration and the exchange of ideas. The synergy of diverse perspectives often sparks creativity and fosters an atmosphere where innovation flourishes.

Collaboration within IT teams, across departments, and even with external partners is essential. IT professionals need to break down silos, share insights, and leverage collective knowledge to address challenges and uncover novel solutions. Through collaborative efforts, IT professionals can harness the power of collective intelligence, pushing the boundaries of what is achievable.

## 3. Empowering a Culture of Risk-Taking

Innovation is inherently linked to risk-taking. IT professionals must be encouraged to step out of their comfort zones, experiment with new approaches, and embrace the possibility of failure. A culture that tolerates calculated risks provides the space for creativity to thrive.

Leaders within the IT industry play a crucial role in fostering this culture. By supporting and recognizing innovative initiatives, they empower IT professionals to explore uncharted territories. Learning from failures becomes an integral part of the innovation process, guiding professionals toward refined solutions and pushing the industry to new heights.

## Challenges on the Innovation Horizon

1. Balancing Security and Innovation

In the era of constant cyber threats, IT professionals face the challenge of balancing innovation with robust security measures. As they explore new technologies, the need for ensuring data integrity, privacy, and protection against cyber threats becomes paramount.

Innovative solutions must not compromise the security of systems and data. IT professionals must navigate the delicate balance between embracing cutting-edge technologies and implementing security measures that safeguard against potential vulnerabilities. This requires a keen understanding of evolving cybersecurity threats and the integration of security measures into the fabric of technological advancements.

2. Overcoming Resistance to Change

Innovation often encounters resistance from those comfortable with existing systems and processes. IT professionals need to navigate this resistance, whether it comes from within their organizations or from end-users. Effective communication and education about the benefits of innovation are crucial to overcoming reluctance to change.

Addressing the human aspect of innovation involves not only introducing new technologies but also facilitating a smooth transition. IT professionals must demonstrate the tangible advantages of innovation, showcasing how it improves efficiency, user experience, and overall business outcomes.

**Examples**

1. Blockchain Revolutionizing Supply Chain Management

Blockchain is a decentralized and distributed digital ledger technology that securely records transactions across a network of computers. It uses cryptographic techniques to ensure transparency, immutability, and trust, making it suitable for various applications, including cryptocurrency transactions, supply chain management, and smart contracts.

Blockchain technology has emerged as a transformative force, and its impact on supply chain management is noteworthy. IT professionals played a pivotal role in conceptualizing and implementing blockchain solutions that enhance transparency, traceability, and security within supply chains.

Through the creative integration of blockchain, IT professionals have enabled businesses to streamline operations, reduce fraud, and build trust among stakeholders. This case exemplifies how innovation in IT can revolutionize traditional industries, paving the way for a more efficient and secure future.

2. Artificial Intelligence in Healthcare Diagnostics

The healthcare industry has witnessed the integration of artificial intelligence (AI) in diagnostics, with IT professionals at the forefront of this revolution. Through the creative application of AI algorithms, medical professionals can analyze vast amounts of data to identify patterns and make accurate diagnoses.

This example highlights the collaborative efforts of IT professionals and healthcare experts, showcasing how the fusion of technology and domain expertise can lead to groundbreaking innovations. The implementation of AI in healthcare diagnostics not only improves the accuracy of diagnoses but also accelerates the pace of medical advancements.

**Conclusion**

As we navigate the complex landscape of IT, the inseparable connection between innovation, creativity, and IT professionals becomes increasingly evident. The industry's future hinges on the ability of IT professionals to embrace continuous learning, foster collaboration, and navigate challenges with resilience and creativity.

Innovation in IT is not a destination but a journey - a continuous evolution that requires adaptability, curiosity, and a willingness to take calculated risks. By understanding the role they play in shaping the technological landscape, IT professionals can chart a course toward a future where innovation and creativity are not just tools but guiding principles in overcoming the challenges of the ever-evolving IT industry.

# Chapter 9. Project Management in the Digital Age

## Introduction

In the dynamic landscape of Information Technology (IT), project management has evolved significantly, especially in the digital age. As technology continues to advance at an unprecedented pace, IT professionals are tasked with delivering complex projects efficiently and effectively. This article delves into the intricacies of project management in the digital age, exploring various methodologies and addressing the unique challenges faced by IT professionals in this ever-evolving domain.

## The Evolution of Project Management Methodologies

### 1. Traditional vs. Agile: Finding the Right Fit

The traditional waterfall approach, characterized by sequential phases, has been the stalwart of project management for decades. However, the digital age has ushered in the era of Agile methodologies, emphasizing adaptability and collaboration. IT professionals must carefully assess the nature of their projects to determine whether a traditional or Agile approach is more suitable.

*Traditional Waterfall Methodology*

The waterfall model follows a linear and sequential process, with distinct phases such as requirements, design, implementation, testing, and maintenance. While this approach provides structure, it can be rigid and less responsive to changing project requirements.

*Agile Methodology*

Agile, on the other hand, promotes iterative development, collaboration, and flexibility. Scrum and Kanban are popular Agile frameworks that enable IT professionals to respond to changes swiftly. Agile methodologies align well with the fast-paced nature of IT projects, allowing for continuous improvement and client feedback.

## 2. Hybrid Approaches for Maximum Flexibility

Recognizing the strengths of both traditional and Agile methodologies, many IT professionals opt for hybrid approaches. By blending the structured nature of waterfall with the adaptive elements of Agile, project managers can tailor their approach to the unique needs of each project. This hybridization offers a balanced framework that accommodates evolving project requirements.

**Project Management Tools in the Digital Age**

## 1. Collaborative Platforms and Communication Tools

In the digital age, project management tools have become indispensable for IT professionals. Collaborative platforms such as Jira, Trello, and Asana facilitate real-time communication, task tracking, and project documentation. These tools enhance team collaboration, streamline workflows, and contribute to overall project transparency.

*Jira: Streamlining Development Workflows*

Jira, a widely used project management tool, is particularly beneficial for software development projects. It enables teams to plan, track, and manage their work with features like Scrum and Kanban boards. Jira's integration capabilities with other development tools enhance the overall efficiency of IT projects.

*Trello: Visualizing Workflows*

Trello's user-friendly interface and visual boards make it a popular choice for project management. IT professionals can create boards for tasks, assign team members, and move cards across different stages of the project. Trello's simplicity and flexibility contribute to its widespread adoption in various IT environments.

*Asana: Enhancing Collaboration and Task Management*

Asana is a versatile project management tool that facilitates collaboration and task management across teams. With features for creating tasks, setting priorities, and tracking progress, Asana helps streamline workflows and improve team coordination. Its user-friendly interface and integration capabilities make it a valuable asset for managing diverse projects in an efficient and organized manner.

## 2. Automation and Artificial Intelligence (AI)

As the digital age unfolds, automation and AI are revolutionizing project management. AI-driven tools analyze historical project data, predict potential risks, and suggest optimal resource allocation. Automation streamlines repetitive tasks, allowing IT professionals to focus on high-value activities and strategic decision-making.

*Risk Management with AI*

AI algorithms can analyze past project data to identify patterns and anticipate potential risks. By leveraging predictive analytics, project managers can proactively address issues, minimizing the impact on project timelines and outcomes. AI-driven risk management enhances project resilience in the face of uncertainties.

*Task Automation for Efficiency*

Automation tools like Zapier and Microsoft Power Automate enable the integration of various applications, automating routine tasks and data transfers. This not only reduces manual effort but also enhances accuracy and consistency in project workflows. IT professionals can leverage automation to ensure seamless collaboration and information flow across different tools.

**Challenges in Project Management for IT Professionals**

1. Dynamic Project Requirements

In the digital age, IT projects often face rapidly changing requirements due to technological advancements, market dynamics, or client feedback. Managing these dynamic requirements requires an agile mindset and flexible project management methodologies. Failure to adapt can result in project delays and dissatisfaction among stakeholders.

2. Cybersecurity Concerns

IT projects, by their nature, involve handling sensitive data and implementing complex systems. Cybersecurity concerns pose a significant challenge, requiring IT professionals to integrate robust security measures throughout the project lifecycle. Addressing cybersecurity proactively is essential to prevent data breaches and protect the integrity of IT projects.

### 3. Talent Acquisition and Retention

The demand for skilled IT professionals has surged in the digital age, leading to intense competition for talent. Project managers face challenges in recruiting and retaining skilled team members, impacting project timelines and success. Strategies such as continuous skill development, mentorship programs, and creating a positive work environment are crucial for addressing this challenge.

### 4. Balancing Speed and Quality

In the fast-paced IT landscape, there is often a pressure to deliver projects quickly without compromising on quality. Striking the right balance between speed and quality is a perennial challenge for IT professionals. Implementing Agile methodologies and automated testing processes can help achieve both speed and high-quality project outcomes.

**Strategies for Success in Digital Project Management**

### 1. Embracing a Culture of Continuous Improvement

To navigate the challenges of digital project management, IT professionals must foster a culture of continuous improvement. Regular retrospectives, feedback loops, and learning from both successes and failures contribute to ongoing enhancements in project management processes. This iterative approach aligns with the principles of Agile methodologies.

## 2. Prioritizing Cybersecurity from the Outset

Given the increasing frequency and sophistication of cyber threats, prioritizing cybersecurity from the project's inception is paramount. Conducting thorough risk assessments, implementing encryption measures, and staying abreast of cybersecurity trends are essential components of a proactive cybersecurity strategy.

## 3. Investing in Training and Development

In the rapidly evolving field of IT, investing in the training and development of project teams is crucial. Ensuring that team members are up-to-date with the latest technologies and methodologies enhances their capabilities to tackle complex projects. This investment not only benefits project outcomes but also contributes to talent retention.

## 4. Creating a Flexible Project Management Framework

Recognizing that no single project management methodology fits all projects, IT professionals should adopt a flexible framework. Whether it's a hybrid approach or the ability to seamlessly switch between methodologies, flexibility ensures adaptability to evolving project requirements and challenges.

## Conclusion

Project management in the digital age demands a delicate balance of flexibility, innovation, and strategic thinking. IT professionals are at the forefront of navigating this landscape, where traditional and Agile methodologies converge, and technologies like AI and automation redefine project management practices. By embracing a culture of continuous improvement, prioritizing cybersecurity, investing in talent development, and adopting flexible frameworks, IT professionals can overcome challenges and lead successful projects in the dynamic world of Information Technology. As the digital age continues to unfold, the role of project management in ensuring the success of IT initiatives remains more crucial than ever.

## Introduction

In recent years, the global workforce has witnessed a paradigm shift with the widespread adoption of remote work. The IT industry, in particular, has been at the forefront of this revolution, transforming the traditional office-based model into a more flexible and dynamic work environment. This article delves into the profound impact of the remote work revolution on IT professionals, examining both the challenges they face and the opportunities it presents.

## The Evolution of Remote Work in IT

The IT landscape has evolved rapidly, driven by advancements in technology and a changing mindset towards work. The remote work revolution can be traced back to the increasing connectivity and collaboration tools that have made it possible for IT professionals to perform their duties seamlessly from anywhere in the world. Cloud computing, *virtualization*, and high-speed internet have become the cornerstones of this transformation.

Virtualization is a technology that allows multiple operating systems and applications to run on a single physical server or hardware platform. It creates virtual instances of resources, such as servers, storage, or networks, enabling efficient use of hardware, improved resource management, and greater flexibility in deploying and managing IT infrastructure. Virtualization plays a crucial role in data centers, cloud computing, and software development environments.

**The Impact on Work-Life Balance**

One of the significant advantages of remote work for IT professionals is the improved work-life balance it offers. The flexibility to choose when and where to work empowers individuals to better manage their personal and professional lives. This newfound balance contributes to increased job satisfaction, reduced stress levels, and improved overall well-being among IT professionals.

**Challenges Faced by IT Professionals in the Remote Work Era**

While remote work brings numerous benefits, it is not without its challenges. IT professionals face unique obstacles in this digital landscape, ranging from technical issues to interpersonal communication barriers. One of the primary challenges is maintaining a robust cybersecurity posture as remote access introduces new vulnerabilities and potential threats to sensitive information.

1. Technical Challenges

*Network Connectivity Issues*: Remote work heavily relies on a stable internet connection. IT professionals often encounter challenges related to network stability, bandwidth limitations, and connectivity issues, impacting their ability to perform critical tasks.

*Hardware Limitations*: The absence of on-site IT support can pose challenges when it comes to addressing hardware issues. Remote IT professionals must navigate hardware problems without the immediate assistance of a physical IT team.

## 2. Communication and Collaboration Challenges

*Virtual Communication Barriers*: Remote work can hinder effective communication, as reliance on virtual platforms may lead to misunderstandings and misinterpretations. IT professionals must adapt to these challenges to ensure seamless collaboration.

*Team Cohesion*: Building a cohesive team becomes more challenging in a remote work setting. The lack of face-to-face interactions can impact team dynamics, making it essential for IT professionals to find alternative ways to foster a sense of unity among team members.

## Overcoming Challenges through Technological Solutions

As the remote work revolution unfolds, IT professionals are leveraging innovative technological solutions to overcome the challenges associated with this transition.

## 1. Cybersecurity Measures

Implementing robust cybersecurity measures is paramount in the remote work era. IT professionals are adopting advanced encryption protocols, multi-factor authentication, and secure virtual private networks (VPNs) to fortify the digital infrastructure against potential threats.

## 2. Collaboration Tools

To enhance communication and collaboration, IT professionals are embracing a plethora of tools such as video conferencing platforms, instant messaging apps, and project management software. These tools not only bridge the virtual communication gap but also facilitate efficient project coordination.

## 3. Remote Support Solutions

Addressing hardware issues remotely is made possible through the use of remote support solutions. IT professionals can troubleshoot and resolve technical problems on users' devices without being physically present, ensuring uninterrupted workflow.

## Opportunities Unleashed by Remote Work

The remote work revolution has opened up a world of opportunities for IT professionals, reshaping the way they approach their roles and responsibilities.

## 1. Global Talent Pool

Remote work eliminates geographical barriers, enabling organizations to tap into a global talent pool. IT professionals can collaborate with colleagues and clients from diverse backgrounds, fostering innovation and a broader perspective within the industry.

## 2. Workforce Diversity and Inclusion

The shift towards remote work promotes inclusivity, allowing IT professionals to contribute to projects without concerns related to physical location or office culture. This inclusivity fosters diversity within teams, leading to a richer and more dynamic work environment.

### 3. Flexibility in Working Models

The traditional 9-to-5 work model is no longer the norm. Remote work provides IT professionals with the flexibility to choose their working hours, accommodating various lifestyles and preferences. This flexibility enhances job satisfaction and contributes to increased productivity.

## Future Trends and the Continued Evolution of Remote Work

As IT professionals continue to adapt to the remote work revolution, several trends are shaping the future of work in the industry.

### 1. Hybrid Work Models

Hybrid work models, combining remote and in-office work, are gaining popularity. IT professionals may split their time between the office and remote locations, striking a balance that maximizes productivity and collaboration.

### 2. Emphasis on Digital Skills

The remote work era places a greater emphasis on digital skills. IT professionals need to stay abreast of technological advancements, ensuring they possess the skills required to navigate the evolving digital landscape.

### 3. Wellness Programs and Mental Health Support

Recognizing the importance of employee well-being, organizations are implementing wellness programs and mental health support initiatives. This acknowledges the unique challenges remote work poses to IT professionals and addresses the need for holistic support.

**Conclusion**

The remote work revolution has ushered in a new era for IT professionals, bringing both challenges and opportunities. While navigating technical and communication hurdles, IT professionals have demonstrated resilience and adaptability in the face of unprecedented change. As the industry continues to evolve, embracing remote work not only enhances work-life balance but also unlocks the potential for a more diverse, inclusive, and globally connected IT community. The challenges encountered along the way are not roadblocks but rather opportunities for growth and innovation, shaping a future where IT professionals thrive in an ever-changing digital landscape.

## Introduction

In the dynamic landscape of Information Technology (IT), professionals are not only tasked with creating cutting-edge solutions but also grapple with a myriad of ethical dilemmas. As technology evolves at an unprecedented pace, the ethical considerations surrounding its development, implementation, and usage become increasingly complex. This article delves into the multifaceted world of ethical challenges faced by IT professionals, exploring the nuanced decisions they encounter in their day-to-day work.

## Data Privacy and Security

In an era dominated by big data and interconnected systems, one of the foremost ethical dilemmas for IT professionals is navigating the delicate balance between data privacy and security. With the ever-growing threats of cyber-attacks and the proliferation of personal information online, IT professionals find themselves at the forefront of safeguarding sensitive data. The ethical responsibility to protect user information while ensuring the functionality of systems can be a daunting task.

## Artificial Intelligence and Bias

The rise of Artificial Intelligence (AI) has brought about unprecedented advancements in automation and decision-making. However, the ethical concerns surrounding AI, particularly bias in algorithms, present a formidable challenge for IT professionals. The algorithms that power AI systems are only as unbiased as the data they are trained on, and mitigating bias requires a nuanced understanding of societal norms and cultural nuances. IT professionals are tasked with identifying and rectifying biases in AI models to ensure fair and just outcomes.

**Social Impact of Technology**

As creators of technology, IT professionals must grapple with the ethical implications of their creations on society. The rapid adoption of new technologies can have profound social impacts, ranging from job displacement due to automation to the exacerbation of existing societal inequalities. Balancing innovation with ethical considerations requires IT professionals to be conscious of the broader implications of their work and advocate for responsible development practices.

**Intellectual Property and Open Source**

The ethical dilemma of intellectual property is a longstanding challenge in the IT industry. IT professionals often find themselves at crossroads when deciding between proprietary software, which may limit access but offers financial incentives, and open-source alternatives that promote collaboration but may lack monetary rewards. Striking the right balance between protecting intellectual property and fostering a culture of open innovation poses a continuous ethical challenge for IT professionals.

**Whistleblowing and Corporate Loyalty**

In an industry where confidentiality is paramount, IT professionals may find themselves facing ethical quandaries related to whistleblowing. When confronted with unethical practices within their organizations, IT professionals must weigh their loyalty to the company against their obligation to expose wrongdoing. Navigating this delicate balance requires a strong ethical compass and an understanding of the potential consequences for both the individual and the organization.

## Globalization and Cultural Sensitivity

The interconnected nature of the IT industry means that professionals often work on global projects with diverse teams. This presents ethical challenges related to cultural sensitivity and the potential clash of ethical norms. IT professionals must navigate differing cultural perspectives on privacy, security, and data usage, recognizing that a one-size-fits-all approach may not align with the values of every stakeholder involved.

## Environmental Sustainability

The environmental impact of IT infrastructure and practices is a growing concern. From energy consumption in data centers to the disposal of electronic waste, IT professionals are increasingly called upon to address the ecological footprint of their work. Balancing the need for high-performance computing with environmentally sustainable practices poses a unique ethical challenge that requires a holistic approach to technology development and deployment.

## User Consent and Transparency

IT professionals are often tasked with designing user interfaces and systems that collect and process user data. Ensuring transparent communication about data collection practices and obtaining informed consent from users is an ethical imperative. Striking a balance between creating user-friendly interfaces and providing comprehensive information about data usage requires a delicate touch, emphasizing the importance of ethical communication in IT design.

**Conclusion**

The life and challenges of IT professionals are intricately woven into the ethical fabric of the digital age. As technology continues to advance, so too will the ethical dilemmas faced by those at the forefront of innovation. Navigating the complex landscape of data privacy, AI bias, societal impact, intellectual property, whistleblowing, cultural sensitivity, environmental sustainability, and user transparency demands a constant commitment to ethical principles. In the face of these challenges, IT professionals play a pivotal role in shaping a digital future that is not only technologically advanced but also ethically sound. The journey is fraught with complexities, but it is through addressing and overcoming these ethical dilemmas that IT professionals contribute to a more responsible and sustainable digital world.

## Introduction

In the fast-paced world of technology, where innovation and evolution are constant companions, the life of an IT professional can be both exhilarating and demanding. However, as the industry continues to thrive, so does the mental health challenges faced by those navigating the intricate landscape of code, deadlines, and perpetual learning. This article delves into the multifaceted realm of mental health in the tech industry, exploring the unique stressors that IT professionals encounter and the strategies essential for coping and support.

## Understanding Mental Health Challenges in Tech

### 1. High Expectations and Perpetual Innovation

The tech industry is synonymous with rapid advancements and unrelenting expectations. IT professionals often find themselves on the frontlines, grappling with the pressure to stay ahead of the curve. The constant demand for innovation can be exhilarating but also overwhelming, leading to stress, burnout, and anxiety.

### 2. Tight Deadlines and Project Pressures

In the dynamic world of IT, tight deadlines and demanding project schedules are par for the course. The pressure to deliver flawless code or meet project milestones can take a toll on mental well-being. Professionals may find themselves caught in a cycle of chronic stress, impacting their overall mental health.

## 3. Isolation and Remote Work Challenges

The rise of remote work, accelerated by technological advancements, has brought about a new set of challenges. IT professionals, who traditionally thrive on collaboration and teamwork, may find themselves isolated in virtual workspaces. This sense of disconnection can contribute to feelings of loneliness and exacerbate existing mental health issues.

## 4. Continuous Learning and Skill Gaps

In an industry where change is the only constant, IT professionals must engage in continuous learning to stay relevant. While this commitment to growth is commendable, the perpetual need to acquire new skills can lead to *imposter syndrome* (a psychological phenomenon wherein individuals doubt their achievements, fear being exposed as a fraud, and attribute their success to luck rather than their own abilities), self-doubt, and a sense of inadequacy, impacting mental well-being.

**Strategies for Coping and Support**

## 1. Promoting a Healthy Work-Life Balance

Recognizing the importance of a healthy work-life balance is crucial in mitigating mental health challenges. Encouraging employees to set boundaries, take breaks, and disconnect from work during non-working hours fosters a more sustainable and supportive work environment.

## 2. Fostering a Culture of Open Communication

Creating a culture where open communication about mental health is encouraged is vital. IT organizations should prioritize destigmatizing discussions around mental health, ensuring that employees feel safe sharing their struggles and seeking support without fear of judgment.

### 3. Providing Mental Health Resources

Offering access to mental health resources, such as counseling services and employee assistance programs, is a proactive step in supporting IT professionals. Recognizing that mental health is an integral part of overall well-being underscores the organization's commitment to the holistic health of its workforce.

### 4. Encouraging Skill Development and Training

To alleviate the pressure associated with skill gaps, organizations can invest in comprehensive training programs. Providing employees with opportunities for skill development not only enhances their capabilities but also instills confidence, reducing the mental strain associated with staying relevant in a rapidly evolving industry.

### 5. Building a Supportive Community

Facilitating connections among IT professionals, both within and outside the organization, can combat feelings of isolation. Peer support groups, mentorship programs, and networking events contribute to a sense of community, fostering a supportive environment where individuals can share experiences and insights.

**Conclusion**

As the tech industry continues to shape the future, the mental well-being of its workforce must be a priority. The challenges faced by IT professionals are complex and multifaceted, requiring a holistic approach to support and coping strategies. By acknowledging the unique stressors inherent in the industry and implementing proactive measures, organizations can cultivate a culture that prioritizes mental health, ensuring that those at the forefront of innovation can navigate the labyrinth of the tech world with resilience and well-being.

## Introduction

In the rapidly evolving landscape of the tech industry, where innovation and progress are paramount, the significance of diversity and inclusion cannot be overstated. This article delves into the pivotal role diversity plays in the IT workplace, exploring its impact on innovation, problem-solving, and overall company success. We will also examine various initiatives that organizations can undertake to promote diversity and inclusion, ensuring a more vibrant and equitable environment for IT professionals.

## Understanding Diversity in Tech

Diversity in the tech industry extends beyond the visible differences such as gender and ethnicity. It encompasses a broad spectrum, including but not limited to age, socioeconomic background, education, and cognitive styles. Recognizing and appreciating this diversity is the first step toward building a resilient and innovative workforce.

## Benefits of Diversity in Driving Innovation

One of the primary advantages of a diverse workforce in the tech industry lies in its ability to drive innovation. Diverse teams bring together individuals with different perspectives, experiences, and problem-solving approaches. This amalgamation of ideas often leads to creative solutions and breakthrough innovations that might elude homogenous teams. Research consistently shows that companies with diverse teams are more likely to introduce new products and services to the market.

## Fostering Inclusive Work Environments

Creating an inclusive work environment is essential for retaining diverse talent in the tech industry. Inclusive workplaces ensure that all employees feel valued and respected, fostering a sense of belonging. This, in turn, enhances job satisfaction and employee retention. When individuals feel their unique contributions are recognized and appreciated, they are more likely to stay engaged and committed to their work.

## Overcoming Unconscious Bias in Hiring and Promotion

Unconscious bias can inadvertently seep into various stages of the hiring and promotion process. To counteract this, organizations need to implement strategies that promote fair and unbiased decision-making. This may involve training hiring managers and decision-makers to recognize and mitigate their biases, ensuring that opportunities are distributed equitably among all employees.

## Promoting Diversity in Leadership Roles

While strides have been made in diversifying entry-level positions, there is still a noticeable gap when it comes to leadership roles in the tech industry. Encouraging diversity in leadership is crucial for creating role models and mentors for underrepresented groups. Organizations should actively seek to identify and nurture diverse talent, providing them with opportunities to climb the corporate ladder.

## Educational Initiatives

To address the lack of diversity in the IT talent pipeline, it is imperative to invest in educational initiatives. This involves partnering with schools and universities to create programs that expose students from underrepresented backgrounds to technology and provide them with the necessary skills. By fostering diversity at the educational level, the industry can cultivate a more inclusive workforce in the long run.

## Mentorship and Networking Programs

Mentorship and networking programs play a pivotal role in the professional development of individuals from underrepresented groups. Establishing formal mentorship programs can help bridge the gap between different career levels, providing guidance and support to diverse talent. Additionally, fostering networking opportunities allows individuals to connect with like-minded professionals, creating a supportive community within the organization.

## Employee Resource Groups

Employee Resource Groups (ERGs) are instrumental in creating communities within organizations that support specific demographic groups. Whether based on gender, ethnicity, or other factors, ERGs provide a platform for employees to connect, share experiences, and advocate for inclusivity. These groups contribute to a more inclusive workplace by fostering a sense of community and amplifying the voices of underrepresented employees.

**Measuring Diversity and Inclusion**

To ensure the effectiveness of diversity and inclusion initiatives, organizations must establish clear metrics and accountability measures. Regularly assessing the diversity of the workforce, tracking progress, and holding leaders accountable for meeting diversity goals are essential steps in creating a culture that values and prioritizes inclusion.

**Conclusion**

Diversity and inclusion are not just buzzwords in the tech industry; they are integral components of a thriving and innovative workplace. By understanding the various dimensions of diversity, fostering inclusive environments, and implementing targeted initiatives, organizations can unlock the full potential of their workforce. As the tech industry continues to shape the future, embracing diversity is not only a moral imperative but a strategic necessity for sustained success and competitiveness. It is through these collective efforts that the IT professionals of tomorrow will navigate and overcome the challenges, contributing to a more diverse, inclusive, and prosperous tech landscape.

## Introduction

The world of information technology (IT) is in a constant state of flux, and IT professionals find themselves at the forefront of groundbreaking changes that shape the way we live, work, and communicate. As we peer into the future of IT jobs, it becomes evident that the landscape is set to undergo transformative shifts, presenting both exciting opportunities and unforeseen challenges for those in the field.

## Rise of Artificial Intelligence and Automation

One of the most significant trends reshaping the IT job market is the pervasive influence of artificial intelligence (AI) and automation. As machines become more adept at handling routine tasks, IT professionals will need to evolve and focus on higher-order skills such as problem-solving, critical thinking, and creativity. Roles in AI development, machine learning, and data science are poised to become increasingly central to IT job portfolios.

## Cloud Computing and the Virtual Workspace

The advent of cloud computing has revolutionized the way businesses operate, enabling seamless collaboration and data accessibility across geographies. This shift towards a virtual workspace demands IT professionals with expertise in cloud architecture, security, and management. Roles related to cloud infrastructure, *DevOps*, and cybersecurity will be in high demand as organizations seek to fortify their digital ecosystems.

DevOps is a set of practices that aims to foster collaboration and communication between software development (Dev) and IT operations (Ops) teams, emphasizing automation, continuous integration, and continuous delivery to achieve faster and more reliable software development and deployment processes.

## Emerging Technologies

Blockchain technology, originally developed for cryptocurrencies, has found applications beyond the financial sector. It is poised to redefine how we secure data and conduct transactions. Similarly, the Internet of Things (IoT) is creating a network of interconnected devices, generating vast amounts of data. IT professionals specializing in blockchain development and IoT management will find themselves in a position to shape the future of these technologies.

## Cybersecurity

As the digital landscape expands, so does the threat landscape. Cybersecurity will remain a paramount concern for businesses and individuals alike. IT professionals specializing in ethical hacking, threat analysis, and security architecture will play a pivotal role in safeguarding sensitive information from malicious actors. The demand for cybersecurity experts is expected to surge as organizations recognize the need for robust defense mechanisms.

## The Evolution of Software Development

The traditional waterfall model of software development is giving way to more agile and iterative approaches. *Continuous integration, continuous delivery* (CI/CD), and

DevOps practices are becoming the norm. Continuous Integration (CI) automates the integration of code changes from multiple contributors into a shared repository, ensuring early detection and resolution of integration issues. Continuous Delivery (CD) extends CI by automatically deploying code changes that pass integration tests to production or staging environments, facilitating a continuous and efficient release process.

IT professionals will need to adapt to this changing paradigm, emphasizing collaboration, adaptability, and a rapid response to evolving user needs. The role of a software developer is no longer confined to coding but extends to ensuring the seamless integration of software into complex systems.

## Data Analytics and Business Intelligence

The era of big data is here, and businesses are increasingly relying on data-driven insights to make informed decisions. IT professionals specializing in data analytics and business intelligence will find themselves at the forefront of this data revolution. The ability to extract meaningful patterns and trends from vast datasets will be a valuable skill, with data scientists and analysts in high demand across industries.

## Remote Work

The COVID-19 pandemic accelerated the adoption of remote work, and its effects are likely to persist in the future. IT professionals need to adapt to this new normal, mastering the tools and technologies that facilitate collaboration in virtual environments. Skills related to remote project management, virtual communication, and cybersecurity for distributed workforces will be crucial in the years to come.

## Globalization and Cross-Cultural Competence

As IT projects become increasingly global in scope, IT professionals must develop cross-cultural competence. Effective communication with diverse teams, understanding different work cultures, and navigating various regulatory environments are becoming essential skills. The ability to work seamlessly in a globally distributed team will be a valuable asset, opening up opportunities for IT professionals to contribute to projects on a global scale.

## Challenges on the Horizon

While the future of IT jobs holds immense promise, it is not without its challenges. Here are some potential hurdles that IT professionals may encounter.

### 1. Skills Gap and Continuous Learning

The rapid pace of technological advancement means that the skills learned today may become obsolete tomorrow. IT professionals must embrace a mindset of continuous learning to stay relevant in their field. The challenge lies in bridging the skills gap and ensuring that the workforce is equipped with the latest tools and knowledge.

### 2. Ethical Considerations in Technology

The ethical implications of technology are gaining prominence, with concerns about data privacy, algorithmic bias, and the responsible use of AI. IT professionals will need to grapple with these ethical considerations, ensuring that technological advancements are aligned with societal values. Balancing innovation with ethical responsibility will be a delicate but crucial task.

## 3. Job Displacement Due to Automation

As automation and AI technologies advance, there is a concern about job displacement in certain sectors. Routine and repetitive tasks may be automated, leading to a shift in the nature of certain IT roles. IT professionals must proactively adapt to these changes, reskilling and upskilling to take on more complex and strategic responsibilities.

## 4. Cybersecurity Threats and Evolving Risks

The cat-and-mouse game between cybersecurity experts and malicious actors continues to escalate. New and sophisticated cyber threats constantly emerge, requiring IT professionals to stay ahead of the curve. The challenge lies in anticipating and mitigating evolving risks, as cybercriminals become more innovative and targeted in their attacks.

## Conclusion

The future of IT jobs promises an exciting journey filled with innovation, challenges, and opportunities. As the IT landscape evolves, professionals in the field must be prepared to adapt, upskill, and embrace new technologies. The ability to navigate the complex interplay of emerging trends, ethical considerations, and global dynamics will define the success of IT professionals in the years to come. By staying agile and proactive, IT professionals can not only thrive in this dynamic environment but also contribute significantly to shaping the future of technology and its impact on society.

## Introduction

In the ever-evolving realm of Information Technology (IT), professionals face a myriad of challenges that demand adaptability, resilience, and a commitment to lifelong learning. This article explores the significance of continuous professional development for IT professionals, delving into the dynamic nature of the field and offering strategies to stay abreast of emerging trends and technologies.

## The Dynamic Landscape of IT

The IT landscape is characterized by rapid technological advancements, making it essential for professionals to embrace a mindset of continuous learning. From artificial intelligence and machine learning to cybersecurity and cloud computing, the scope of IT is vast and ever-expanding. Adapting to these changes is not merely a choice but a necessity for those looking to thrive in their careers.

## Lifelong Learning

Lifelong learning is the cornerstone of success in the IT industry. Unlike other fields, where static knowledge might suffice for extended periods, IT professionals must commit to a perpetual cycle of learning to remain relevant. The ability to acquire new skills, assimilate knowledge, and apply it effectively is a hallmark of a successful IT career.

**Embracing a Growth Mindset**

A growth mindset is crucial for IT professionals as they navigate the challenges of continuous learning. This mindset, as coined by psychologist Carol Dweck, involves viewing challenges as opportunities for growth rather than insurmountable obstacles. Embracing a growth mindset fosters a culture of curiosity, adaptability, and resilience, traits essential for success in the IT landscape.

**The Importance of Continuous Professional Development**

Continuous professional development (CPD) is a strategic approach to learning that goes beyond traditional education. It involves ongoing skill enhancement, staying updated with industry trends, and actively seeking opportunities for growth. CPD is a proactive response to the rapidly changing nature of the IT field, ensuring that professionals remain valuable assets to their organizations.

**Strategies for Staying Updated**

1. Engage in Online Courses and Certifications

The digital era has brought forth a plethora of online courses and certifications tailored to IT professionals. Platforms like Coursera, edX, and LinkedIn Learning offer a diverse range of courses, enabling individuals to upskill and specialize in specific areas. Engaging with these resources allows IT professionals to acquire new knowledge at their own pace.

## 2. Attend Conferences and Workshops

Participating in conferences and workshops is an excellent way to stay updated on the latest trends, network with industry experts, and gain hands-on experience. Events such as AWS re:Invent, and Microsoft Ignite provide valuable insights into emerging technologies and best practices, fostering a sense of community among IT professionals.

## 3. Join Professional Associations and Forums

Being part of professional associations and forums within the IT community provides a platform for networking, knowledge exchange, and mentorship. Associations like the Association for Computing Machinery (ACM) and forums like Stack Overflow facilitate discussions, problem-solving, and the sharing of experiences, contributing to continuous professional development.

## 4. Establish a Personal Learning Network (PLN)

A Personal Learning Network (PLN) is a curated collection of individuals and resources that aid in professional growth. Through social media platforms, forums, and online communities, IT professionals can build and nurture their PLNs. This enables the exchange of ideas, collaborative learning, and the discovery of new opportunities for skill development.

**Balancing Practical Experience with Theoretical Knowledge**

While theoretical knowledge is crucial, practical experience is equally vital in the IT field. Striking a balance between hands-on experience and theoretical understanding ensures a holistic approach to learning. Practical application of knowledge reinforces understanding and equips IT professionals to address real-world challenges effectively.

**Mentorship and Knowledge Transfer**

Mentorship plays a pivotal role in the professional development of IT enthusiasts. Experienced mentors provide valuable insights, guidance, and a roadmap for career progression. Additionally, knowledge transfer within teams fosters a collaborative learning environment, where seasoned professionals share their expertise with colleagues, ensuring the continuity of knowledge within the organization.

**Overcoming Challenges in Continuous Learning**

1. Time Management

One of the primary challenges in continuous learning is time management. IT professionals often juggle demanding work schedules and personal commitments. Effective time management strategies, such as setting realistic goals, prioritizing tasks, and dedicating specific time slots for learning, are essential for overcoming this challenge.

2. Information Overload

The IT landscape is inundated with information, making it challenging to discern relevant content. Developing critical thinking skills and leveraging curated learning resources help filter information, ensuring that professionals focus on what is most pertinent to their areas of expertise.

Some IT professionals may resist embracing new technologies or methodologies due to a fear of change. Overcoming this resistance involves cultivating a growth mindset, emphasizing the benefits of adaptation, and creating a culture that encourages experimentation and innovation.

**Conclusion**

In the dynamic and fast-paced world of IT, learning is not a phase but a perpetual journey. Continuous professional development is not only about staying relevant but also about thriving amidst challenges. By embracing a growth mindset, actively participating in CPD activities, and overcoming common challenges, IT professionals can navigate the complexities of their field with confidence, ensuring a fulfilling and successful career.

## Introduction

In the fast-paced world of Information Technology (IT), professionals find themselves at the forefront of innovation and change. The dynamic nature of the industry comes with a unique set of challenges, often taking a toll on personal relationships. This article delves into the intricate web of how an IT career impacts personal relationships, examining the stressors, communication challenges, and strategies to maintain a healthy balance between professional ambitions and personal connections.

## The Demands of an IT Career

### 1. Time Constraints and Work-Life Balance

One of the primary challenges IT professionals face is the demanding nature of their work, often requiring long hours and late-night troubleshooting sessions. The perpetual need to stay ahead in a rapidly evolving field can make it challenging to strike a balance between professional commitments and personal life. The blurred lines between work and personal time can strain relationships, as partners may feel neglected or secondary to the demands of the job.

### 2. High Stress Levels and Emotional Exhaustion

The high-pressure environment of the IT industry can lead to elevated stress levels and emotional exhaustion. Constant deadlines, problem-solving, and the weight of responsibility can affect an individual's mental well-being.

When stress spills over into personal life, it may lead to mood swings, irritability, and strained interactions with loved ones. Understanding the toll of stress on personal relationships is crucial for IT professionals aiming to foster a healthy home environment.

**Communication Challenges**

1. Technical Jargon and Communication Gaps

IT professionals often find themselves immersed in a world of technical jargon and complex concepts that may be difficult for non-technical partners to grasp. Effective communication is key to any relationship, and the challenge lies in translating intricate IT issues into understandable language. Miscommunication due to technical gaps can lead to frustration and misunderstandings, highlighting the need for IT professionals to hone their communication skills outside the workplace.

2. Remote Work Challenges

The rise of remote work, accelerated by technological advancements, has become a double-edged sword for IT professionals. While it offers flexibility, it can also lead to isolation and a lack of physical boundaries between work and personal life. Remote work may exacerbate the challenges of maintaining a healthy work-life balance, as the home environment becomes both an office and a personal space. Navigating the complexities of remote work requires proactive communication with partners and establishing clear boundaries.

## Strategies for Maintaining a Healthy Balance

### 1. Prioritizing Self-Care and Well-being

To navigate the demands of an IT career and its impact on personal relationships, prioritizing self-care is essential. IT professionals should recognize the signs of burnout and stress, taking proactive steps to manage their mental and physical well-being. Regular exercise, adequate sleep, and mindfulness practices can contribute to a healthier mindset, fostering resilience in the face of professional challenges.

### 2. Setting Boundaries and Managing Time Effectively

Establishing clear boundaries between work and personal life is crucial for maintaining a healthy balance. IT professionals should communicate their working hours to their partners and strive to adhere to them. This not only helps in managing expectations but also creates dedicated time for personal relationships. Effective time management, including prioritizing tasks and avoiding unnecessary overtime, contributes to a more balanced and fulfilling life.

### 3. Improving Communication Skills

Recognizing the communication challenges inherent in the IT profession, professionals should actively work on improving their communication skills. This involves developing the ability to explain technical concepts in layman's terms and actively listening to partners' concerns. Regular check-ins and open conversations about the challenges and successes at work foster mutual understanding and support.

Building a support system within personal relationships is crucial for weathering the storms of an IT career. Partners who understand the demands of the profession and offer emotional support can be invaluable. Creating a sense of shared goals and mutual understanding helps strengthen the bond, making it easier to navigate the challenges that come with the territory.



In the face of time constraints, IT professionals must prioritize quality over quantity when it comes to spending time with loved ones. Allocating focused, undistracted time for personal connections enhances the quality of relationships. Whether it's a weekend getaway, a shared hobby, or simply enjoying a meal together, these moments become anchors in a relationship, providing much-needed respite from the demands of the IT world.

**Conclusion**

As IT professionals continue to shape the future through technological innovation, the impact on personal relationships cannot be overlooked. The challenges of time constraints, communication gaps, and high stress levels necessitate a proactive approach to maintaining a healthy balance. By prioritizing self-care, improving communication skills, and fostering supportive relationships, IT professionals can navigate the complexities of their careers while nurturing meaningful connections outside the realm of code and algorithms. In doing so, they not only fortify their personal lives but also contribute to a more sustainable and fulfilling professional journey.

## Introduction

In the fast-paced and dynamic world of Information Technology (IT), professionals find themselves at the forefront of innovation, shaping the landscape of the digital era. As technology continues to permeate every aspect of our lives, the social responsibility of IT professionals becomes increasingly paramount. This article explores the multifaceted role of IT professionals in addressing societal issues, examining ethical responsibilities, and contributing to positive societal change.

## The Evolving Landscape of IT

The IT industry is marked by constant evolution, with professionals adapting to new technologies and methodologies. This dynamism brings with it a unique set of challenges and opportunities for IT professionals to contribute meaningfully to society.

### 1. Innovation and Social Impact

Innovation in IT has the power to drive positive social change. IT professionals are at the forefront of developing solutions that address critical societal issues, ranging from healthcare to education. For instance, the advent of telemedicine and e-learning platforms has transformed accessibility, making healthcare and education more inclusive and reaching underserved populations.

With concerns about climate change on the rise, IT professionals are increasingly called upon to contribute to environmental sustainability. Data centers, which are the backbone of digital infrastructure, are notorious for their energy consumption. IT professionals are tasked with developing energy-efficient solutions, implementing *green computing practices*, and promoting sustainable IT infrastructure to minimize the industry's environmental footprint.

Green computing practices refer to environmentally sustainable approaches in information technology that aim to reduce the environmental impact of computing operations. These practices may include energy-efficient hardware, responsible disposal of electronic waste, virtualization to optimize resource utilization, and the use of renewable energy sources to power data centers. The goal is to minimize the ecological footprint of computing activities and promote a more environmentally friendly IT industry.

## Ethical Responsibilities of IT Professionals

As technology becomes deeply integrated into daily life, IT professionals must grapple with ethical considerations that arise from their work.

### 1. Data Privacy and Security

One of the foremost ethical concerns in the IT industry revolves around data privacy and security. IT professionals handle vast amounts of sensitive information, and breaches can have severe consequences for individuals and organizations. Upholding the principles of privacy and security requires IT professionals to implement robust measures, stay abreast of evolving threats, and advocate for ethical data practices within their organizations.

2. Bias in Artificial Intelligence (AI) and Algorithms

The increasing use of AI and machine learning algorithms raises concerns about bias in decision-making processes. IT professionals play a crucial role in identifying and mitigating bias within algorithms to ensure fair and equitable outcomes. Recognizing the ethical implications of their work, IT professionals must advocate for transparency, accountability, and inclusivity in the development and deployment of AI systems.

## Bridging the Digital Divide

The digital divide persists as a significant societal challenge, with disparities in access to technology and information. IT professionals have a responsibility to bridge this gap, ensuring that technology is accessible to all.

1. Inclusive Design and Accessibility

IT professionals can contribute to social responsibility by championing inclusive design principles. Creating technology that is accessible to individuals with diverse abilities ensures that the benefits of technological advancements are enjoyed by everyone. From developing user interfaces with accessibility features to advocating for accessibility standards, IT professionals can make a substantial impact in fostering inclusivity.

To address the digital divide, IT professionals should actively engage with local communities and contribute to educational initiatives. Providing training and resources to underserved populations empowers individuals to leverage technology for personal and professional growth. By sharing their knowledge, IT professionals can act as catalysts for positive change, fostering a more inclusive and equitable digital society.

## Corporate Social Responsibility (CSR) in IT

As IT companies wield significant influence in the global economy, the concept of Corporate Social Responsibility (CSR) becomes increasingly relevant.

### 1. Sustainable Practices

IT professionals can advocate for and implement sustainable business practices within their organizations. This includes reducing electronic waste, adopting eco-friendly technologies, and supporting environmentally responsible supply chain practices. By incorporating sustainability into business strategies, IT companies can contribute to broader environmental goals.

### 2. Philanthropy and Social Initiatives

IT professionals can influence corporate decision-making by promoting philanthropy and social initiatives. This may involve supporting local community projects, contributing to educational programs, or participating in initiatives that address pressing societal issues. By aligning corporate goals with social responsibility, IT professionals can demonstrate the industry's commitment to making a positive impact beyond technology innovation.

**Professional Development and Advocacy**

To fulfill their social responsibility, IT professionals should continually invest in their professional development and actively advocate for ethical and responsible practices within the industry.

1. Continuous Learning and Adaptation

Given the rapid evolution of technology, IT professionals must commit to continuous learning. Staying informed about emerging trends, ethical considerations, and best practices allows them to navigate the complex landscape of IT responsibly. Professional development ensures that IT professionals remain well-equipped to address new challenges and contribute meaningfully to societal advancements.

2. Advocacy for Ethical Standards

Beyond their individual efforts, IT professionals can advocate for industry-wide ethical standards. Participating in professional organizations, conferences, and forums allows them to collaborate with peers in establishing and promoting ethical guidelines. By collectively advocating for responsible practices, IT professionals can contribute to a culture of ethical awareness and accountability within the IT community.

**Conclusion**

The social responsibility of IT professionals extends far beyond the code they write or the systems they manage. As architects of the digital future, IT professionals have the power to shape a more inclusive, ethical, and sustainable society. By embracing their role as catalysts for positive change, IT professionals can navigate the challenges of the digital age while actively contributing to the betterment of humanity. As the IT industry continues to evolve, the social responsibility of IT professionals remains a guiding principle for a future where technology serves the greater good.

As we embark on the final chapter of our journey through the intricate landscape of the life and challenges of IT professionals, it is only fitting to reflect on the extraordinary evolution of the IT industry and the resilient individuals who navigate its complexities. The preceding chapters have guided us through the annals of the digital age, the rise of IT as a profession, the dynamic tech landscape, and the delicate balancing act between work and life. We have explored the essential skills and agile mindset required in the modern IT professional, confronted the ever-evolving realm of cybersecurity, and delved into the crucial realms of innovation, project management, and the remote work revolution.

Ethical dilemmas and the impact of IT on mental health were not ignored, and we've underscored the importance of diversity, inclusion, and the social responsibility of IT professionals. Speculating on the future of IT jobs, we peered into the crystal ball of emerging roles and potential challenges. Learning and continuous professional development were emphasized, along with a consideration of the profound impact of an IT career on personal relationships.

Now, in this concluding chapter, we grapple with the overarching theme of navigating the future - a future fraught with challenges, uncertainties, and rapid technological advancements. Yet, embedded within these challenges are opportunities for growth, innovation, and positive transformation. As we confront the road ahead, the principles of resilience and purpose stand as beacons guiding IT professionals through the complexities of an ever-changing landscape.

## Resilience in the Face of Technological Disruption

The IT industry is no stranger to disruption. From the advent of personal computing to the rise of the internet and the subsequent explosion of mobile technology, each wave of innovation has reshaped the professional landscape for IT professionals. The future promises more of the same, with artificial intelligence, blockchain, quantum computing, and other transformative technologies poised to redefine the very nature of work.

In navigating this technological turbulence, resilience emerges as a cornerstone of professional success. IT professionals must cultivate an adaptive mindset, embracing change as an inevitable part of their journey. Resilience empowers individuals to bounce back from setbacks, learn from failures, and thrive in the face of uncertainty.

Moreover, resilience is not solely an individual attribute but a collective one. Organizations that foster a culture of resilience provide their IT professionals with the support and resources needed to weather storms and emerge stronger. This requires proactive measures such as continuous training, mentorship programs, and a commitment to staying at the forefront of technological advancements.

## Purpose as a Guiding Star

While resilience helps IT professionals weather the storms, purpose provides the compass directing their efforts. Purpose goes beyond mere job satisfaction; it encapsulates a profound sense of meaning and contribution to something greater than oneself. In the dynamic and often demanding world of IT, finding purpose can be the North Star that guides professionals through challenges and triumphs alike.

For IT professionals, purpose can manifest in various forms - from solving complex problems to contributing to groundbreaking innovations. Purpose-driven individuals are more likely to stay committed to their chosen path, even in the face of adversity. As organizations increasingly recognize the value of purpose-driven work cultures, fostering a sense of meaning becomes not just a personal endeavor but a strategic imperative.

**The Interplay of Resilience and Purpose**

Resilience and purpose are not mutually exclusive; in fact, they are intertwined in a symbiotic dance that empowers IT professionals to navigate the future with confidence. A resilient individual, facing the challenges posed by rapid technological change, draws strength from a clear sense of purpose. Purpose, in turn, is fortified by resilience - the ability to adapt, learn, and persevere in the pursuit of meaningful goals.

In essence, the interplay of resilience and purpose creates a dynamic synergy that transforms challenges into opportunities and setbacks into stepping stones. As IT professionals confront the uncertainties of the future, this dynamic duo becomes their most potent ally.

**Strategies for Cultivating Resilience and Purpose**

Continuous Learning: The pace of technological change demands a commitment to lifelong learning. IT professionals must embrace a mindset of continuous improvement, staying abreast of emerging technologies and industry trends.

Mentorship Programs: Both individuals and organizations can benefit from mentorship programs. Experienced mentors can provide guidance, share insights from their own experiences, and offer a valuable support system during challenging times.

Cultivating a Positive Work Culture: Organizations play a pivotal role in fostering resilience and purpose. A positive work culture that values employee well-being, recognizes accomplishments, and encourages collaboration contributes to a sense of purpose and belonging.

Aligning Individual Goals with Organizational Mission: IT professionals find purpose when their individual goals align with the broader mission of the organization. Clear communication of organizational values and goals helps employees see the impact of their work on a larger scale.

Mindfulness and Well-being Initiatives: Incorporating mindfulness and well-being initiatives into the workplace can enhance resilience. From mental health support programs to activities that promote work-life balance, organizations can create environments that prioritize the holistic well-being of their IT professionals.

**Conclusion: Navigating the Future with Confidence**

As we conclude our exploration of the life and challenges of IT professionals, the future unfolds as a landscape of endless possibilities. The digital age, with its rapid advancements and transformative technologies, offers both unprecedented challenges and unparalleled opportunities. In this complex terrain, resilience and purpose emerge as the guiding principles that empower IT professionals to navigate with confidence.

The journey does not end here; it evolves. As we contemplate the future, we recognize that the resilience and purpose cultivated today will shape the IT landscape of tomorrow. Each IT professional, equipped with the tools of adaptation and driven by a sense of purpose, becomes a beacon of innovation, a champion of progress, and a guardian of the digital realm.

In the grand tapestry of the IT profession, where lines of code weave the fabric of our interconnected world, the chapters we've explored collectively contribute to a narrative of growth, challenge, and triumph. The story continues, and the future beckons - a future where IT professionals, armed with resilience and purpose, confront challenges as catalysts for positive change.

"Life and Challenges of IT Professionals" provides an insightful journey into the dynamic realm of Information Technology, unraveling the intricacies of the profession and the individuals who drive its evolution. We embark on a comprehensive exploration of the digital age, tracing the rise of IT professionals from its inception to the present day. The book encompasses a broad spectrum of topics, from the ever-evolving tech landscape and the challenges of maintaining work-life balance in the interconnected world, to the crucial skills and agility demanded by the modern IT professional.

Engaging chapters delve into cybersecurity threats, the fostering of innovation, the intricacies of project management, and the transformative impact of the remote work revolution. Ethical considerations, mental health challenges, and the imperative of diversity and inclusion are addressed, emphasizing the broader societal responsibilities of IT professionals. The book concludes with a forward-looking gaze into the future of IT jobs, emphasizing the importance of continuous professional development and the impact of an IT career on personal relationships. It is not only a resource for IT professionals navigating the challenges of their field but also an insightful guide for anyone intrigued by the fascinating intersection of technology and human experiences.

# ABOUT THE AUTHOR

**Mr. C. P. Kumar** is a retired Scientist 'G' from National Institute of Hydrology, Roorkee, Uttarakhand, India. He is also a Reiki Healer and Chakra Balancing practitioner (with pendulum dowsing) and offers Emotional Freedom Technique (EFT) to help individuals with emotional issues. Mr. Kumar has authored many books on technical, spiritual, and social topics.

For further details, you may visit his webpage
https://www.angelfire.com/nh/cpkumar/virgo.html